The
Bridge Between
Universal Spirituality
and the
Physical Constitution
of Man

The
Bridge Between
Universal Spirituality
and the
Physical Constitution
of Man

Three Lectures by
Rudolf Steiner

Anthroposophic Press

The three lectures presented here were given December 17-19, 1920 in
Dornach, Switzerland. They are included in *Die Bruecke zwischen der
Weltgeistigkeit und dem Physichen des Menschen.*
(Vol. 202 in the Bibliographic Survey, 1961)

Translated from the original German
by Dorothy S. Osmond.

ISBN 978-0-910142-03-8

ARCHIVE
EDITION

Contents

but man's moral thinking imbues life into substance and will.—The natural world dies away in man; in the realm of the moral a new natural world comes into being; thus are the moral order and the natural order connected.—Absence of spirituality in the modern picture of the world which is based on the Copernican system.— Kepler and Newton.—We need a spiritual view of the universe.—The sun is not a globe of burning gas but the reflection of a spiritual reality revealed in the physical.—The moral power developed by man rays out and is reflected as the spiritual Sun.—Julian the Apostate.—The connection of the spiritual Sun with the physical sun is the Christ-Secret.

DECEMBER 18, 1920.

Man as a being of Thinking, Action and Feeling.—The connection of the life of thought with the will.—Pure thinking: irradiation of the life of thought by will.—This leads to Freedom.—Irradiation of the life of will by thoughts leads to Love.—The meaning of the ancient expressions: Semblance, Power, Wisdom.—To speak of the imperishability of matter and energy annuls Love.—The significance of Freedom and Love in world-happenings.

DECEMBER 19, 1920.

I

Soul and Spirit in Man's Physical Constitution

Today I want to interpolate a theme which may possibly seem to you somewhat remote, but it will be of importance for the further development of subjects we are studying at the present time. We have been able to gather together many details which are essential for a knowledge of man's being. On the one side, we are gradually discovering man's place in the life of the cosmos, and on the other, his place in the social life. But it will be necessary today to consider certain matters which make for a better understanding of man's being and nature.

When man is studied by modern scientific thinking, one part only of his being is taken into consideration. No account whatever is taken of the fact that in addition to his physical body, man also has higher members. But we will leave this aside today and think about something that is more or less recognized in science and has also made its way into the general consciousness.

In studying the human being, only those elements which can be pictured as solid, or solid-fluidic, are regarded as belonging to his organism. It is, of course, acknowledged that the fluid and the aeriform elements

7

pass into and out of the human being, but these are not in themselves considered to be integral members of the human organism. The warmth within man which is greater than that of his environment is regarded as a state or condition of his organism, but not as an actual member of his constitution. We shall presently see what I mean by saying this. I have already drawn attention to the fact that when we study the rising and falling of the cerebral fluid through the spinal canal, we can observe a regular up-and-down oscillatory movement caused by inhalation and exhalation; when we breathe in, the cerebral fluid is driven upwards and strikes, as it were, against the brain-structure; when we breathe out the fluid sinks again. These processes in the purely liquid components of the human organism are not considered to be part and parcel of the organism itself. The general idea is that man, as a physical structure, consists of the more or less solid, or at most solid-fluid, substances found in him.

Man is pictured as a structure built up from these

I.

more or less solid substances (diagram I). The other elements, the fluid element, as I have shown by the example of the cerebral fluid, and the aeriform element, are not regarded by anatomy and physiology as belonging to the human organism as such. It is said: Yes, the human being draws in the air which follows certain paths in his body and also has certain definite functions. This air is breathed out again.—Then people speak of the warmth-condition of the body, but in reality they regard the solid element as the only organizing factor and do not realize that in addition to this solid structure they should also see the whole man as a column of fluid (blue), as a being permeated with air (red)

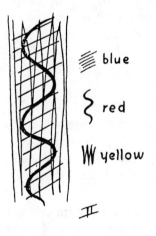

and as a being in whom there is a definite degree of warmth (yellow). More exact study shows that just as the solid or solid-fluid constituents are to be considered as an integral part or member of the organism, so the actual fluidity should not be thought of as so much uniform fluid, but as being differentiated and organized—though the process here is a more fluctuating one—and having its own particular significance.

In addition to the solid man, therefore, we must bear in mind the 'fluid man' and also the 'aeriform man.' For the air that is within us, in regard to its organization and its differentiations, is an organism in the same sense as the solid organism, only it is gaseous, aeriform, and in motion. And finally, the warmth in us is not a uniform warmth extending over the whole human being, but is also delicately organized. As soon, however, as we begin to speak of the fluid organism which fills the same space that is occupied by the solid organism, we realize immediately that we cannot speak of this fluid organism in earthly man without speaking of the etheric body which permeates this fluid organism and fills it with forces. The physical organism exists for itself, as it were; it is the physical body; in so far as we consider it in its entirety, we regard it, to begin with, as a solid organism. This is the physical body.

We then come to consider the fluid organism which cannot, of course, be investigated in the same way as the solid organism, by dissection, but which must be conceived as an inwardly mobile, fluidic organism. It cannot be studied unless we think of it as permeated by the etheric body.

Thirdly, there is the aeriform organism which again cannot be studied unless we think of it as permeated with forces by the astral body.

Fourthly, there is the warmth-organism with all its inner differentiation. It is permeated by the forces of the Ego.—That is how man as earthly man today is constituted.

Physical organism: Physical body

Man regarded in a different way:

1) Solid organism   Physical body
2) Fluid organism   Etheric body
3) Aeriform organism   Astral body
4) Warmth-organism   Ego

Let us think, for example, of the blood. Inasmuch as it is mainly fluid, inasmuch as this blood belongs to the fluid organism, we find in the blood the etheric body which permeates it with its forces. But in the blood there is also present what is generally called the warmth-condition. But that 'organism' is by no means identical with the organism of the fluid blood as such. If we were to investigate this—and it can also be done with physical methods of investigation—we should find in registering the warmth in the different parts of the human organism that the warmth cannot be identified with the fluid organism or with any other.

Directly we reflect about man in this way we find that it is impossible for our thought to come to a standstill within the limits of the human organism itself. We can remain within these limits only if we are thinking merely of the solid organism which is shut off by the skin from what is outside it. Even this, however, is only apparently so. The solid structure is generally regarded as if it were a firm, self-enclosed block; but it is also inwardly differentiated and is related in manifold ways to the solid earth as a whole. This is obvious from the fact that the different solid substances have, for example, different weights; this alone shows that the solids within the human organism are differentiated, have different specific weights in man. In regard to his physical organism, therefore, the human being is related to the earth as a whole. Nevertheless

11

it is possible, according at least to external evidence, to place spatial limits around the physical organism.

It is different when we come to the second, the fluid organism that is permeated by the etheric body. This fluid organism cannot be strictly demarcated from the environment. Whatever is fluid in any area of space adjoins the fluidic element in the environment. Although the fluid element as such is present in the world outside us in a rarefied state, we cannot make such a definite demarcation between the fluid element within man and the fluid element outside man, as in the case of the solid organism. The boundary between man's inner fluid organism and the fluid element in the external world must therefore be left indefinite.

This is even more emphatically the case when we come to consider the aeriform organism which is permeated by the forces of the astral body. The air within us at a certain moment was outside us a moment before, and it will soon be outside again. We are drawing in and giving out the aeriform element all the time. We can really think only of the air as such which surrounds our earth, and say: it penetrates into our organism and withdraws again; but by penetrating into our organism it becomes an integral part of us. In our aeriform organism we actually have something that constantly builds itself up out of the whole atmosphere and then withdraws again into the atmosphere. Whenever we breathe in, something is built up within us, or, at the very least, each indrawn breath causes a change, a modification, in an upbuilding process within us. Similarly, a destructive, partially destructive, process takes place whenever we breathe out. Our aeriform organism undergoes a certain change with every indrawn breath; it is not exactly newly

12

born, but it undergoes a change, both when we breathe in and when we breathe out. When we breathe out, the aeriform organism does not, of course, die, it merely undergoes a change; but there is constant interaction between the aeriform organism within us and the air outside. The usual trivial conceptions of the human organism can only be due to the failure to realize that there is but a slight degree of difference between the aeriform organism and the solid organism.

And now we come to the warmth-organism. It is of course quite in keeping with materialistic-mechanistic thought to study only the solid organism and to ignore the fluid organism, the aeriform organism, and the warmth-organism. But no real knowledge of man's being can be acquired unless we are willing to acknowledge this membering into a warmth-organism, an aeriform organism, a fluid organism, and an earth-organism (solid).

The warmth-organism is paramountly the field of the Ego. The Ego itself is that spirit-organization which imbues with its own forces the warmth that is within us, and governs and gives it configuration, not only externally but also inwardly. We cannot understand the life and activity of the soul unless we remember that the Ego works directly upon the warmth. It is primarily the Ego in man which activates the will, generates impulses of will.—How does the Ego generate impulses of will? From a different point of view we have spoken of how impulses of will are connected with the earthly sphere, in contrast to the impulses of thought and ideation which are connected with forces outside and beyond the earthly sphere. But how does the Ego, which holds together the impulses of will, send these impulses into the organism, into the whole being of man? This is achieved through the fact that the will works primarily in the warmth-organism. An impulse of will proceeding from the Ego works upon man's warmth-organism. Under present earthly conditions it is not possible for what I shall now describe to you to be there as a concrete reality. Nevertheless it can be envisaged as something that is essentially present in man. It can be envisaged if we disregard the physical organization within the space bounded by the human skin. We disregard this, also the fluid organism, and the aeriform organism. The space then remains filled with nothing but warmth, which is, of course, in communication with the warmth outside. But what is active in this warmth, what sets it in flow, stirs it into movement, makes it into an organism—is the *Ego*.

The astral body of man contains within it the forces of feeling. The astral body brings these forces of feeling into physical operation in man's aeriform organism.

As an earthly being, man's constitution is such that, by way of the warmth-organism, his Ego gives rise to what comes to expression when he acts in the world as a being of will. The feelings experienced in the astral body and coming to expression in the earthly organization manifest as the aeriform organism. And when we come to the etheric organism, to the etheric body, we find within it the *conceptual* process, in so far as this has a pictorial character— more strongly pictorial than we are consciously aware of to begin with, for the physical body still intrudes and tones down the pictures into mental concepts. This process works upon the fluid organism.

This shows us that by taking these different organisms in man into account we come nearer to the life of *soul*. Materialistic observation, which stops short at the solid structure and insists that in the very nature of things water cannot become an organism, is bound to confront the life of soul with complete lack of understanding; for it is precisely in these other organisms that the life of soul comes to immediate expression. The solid organism itself is, in reality, only that which provides support for the other organisms. The solid organism stands there as a supporting structure composed of bones, muscles, and so forth. Into this supporting structure is membered the fluid organism with its own inner differentiation and configuration; in this fluid organism vibrates the etheric body, and within this fluid organism the thoughts are produced. How are the thoughts produced? Through the fact that within the fluid organism something asserts itself in a particular metamorphosis—namely, what we know in the external world as *tone*.

Tone is, in reality, something that leads the ordinary mode of observation very much astray. As earthly human beings we perceive the tone as being borne to us by the air. But in point of fact the air is only the transmitter of the tone, which actually weaves in the air. And anyone who assumes that the tone in its essence is merely a matter of air-vibrations is like a person who says: Man has only his physical organism, and there is no soul in it. If the air-vibrations are thought to constitute the essence of the tone, whereas they are in truth merely its external expression, this is the same as seeing only man's physical organism with no soul in it. The tone which lives in the air is essentially an *etheric* reality. And the tone we hear by way of the air arises through the fact that the air is pervaded by the *Tone-Ether* (see diagram III)

15

III

which is the same as the *Chemical Ether*. In pervading the air, this Chemical Ether imparts what lives within it to the air, and we become aware of what we call the tone.

This Tone-Ether or Chemical Ether is essentially active in our fluid organism. We can therefore make the following distinction: In our fluid organism lives our own etheric body; but in addition there penetrates into it (the fluid organism) from every direction the Tone-Ether which underlies the tone. Please distinguish carefully here. We have within us our etheric body; it works and is active by giving rise to thoughts in our fluid organism. But what may be called the Chemical Ether continually streams in and out of our fluid organism. Thus we have an etheric organism complete in itself, consisting of Chemical Ether, Warmth-Ether, Light-Ether, Life-Ether, and in addition we find in it, in a very special sense, the Chemical Ether which streams in and out by way of the fluid organism.

The astral body which comes to expression in feeling operates through the air organism. But still another kind of Ether by which the air is permeated is connected especially with the air organism. It is the Light-Ether. Earlier conceptions of the world always emphasized this affinity of the outspreading physical air with the Light-Ether which pervades it. This Light-Ether that is borne, as it were, by the air and is related to the air even more intimately than tone, also penetrates into our air organism, and it underlies what there passes into and out of it. Thus we have our astral body which is the bearer of feeling, is especially active in the air organism, and is in constant contact there with the Light-Ether.

And now we come to the Ego. This human Ego, which by way of the will is active in the warmth-organism, is again connected with the outer warmth, with the instreaming and outstreaming Warmth-Ether.

Now consider the following. The etheric body remains in us also during sleep, from the moment of falling asleep to the moment of waking; therefore the interworking between the Chemical Ether and the etheric body continues within our being, via the fluid organism, also while we are asleep. It is different in the case of the astral body and feeling. From the moment of falling asleep to the moment of waking, the astral body is outside the human organism; the astral body and feeling do not then work upon the air organism, but the air organism that is connected with the whole surrounding world—is sustained from outside during sleep. And the human being himself, with his astral body and feeling, goes out of his body and passes into a world with which he is related primarily through the Light-Ether. While

17

he is asleep man lives directly in an element that is transmitted to his astral body by the air organism during waking life. We can speak in a similar way of the Ego and the warmth-organism.

It is obvious from this that an understanding of man's connection with the surrounding universe is possible only as the result of thorough study of these members of his being, of which ordinary, mechanistic thinking takes no account at all. But everything in man interpenetrates, and because the Ego is in the warmth-organism, it also permeates the air organism, the fluid organism, and the solid organism, it permeates them with the warmth which is all-pervading. Thus the warmth-organism lives within the air organism; the warmth-organism, permeated as it is with the forces of the Ego, also works in the fluid organism.

This indicates how, for example, we should look for the way in which the Ego works in the circulating blood. It works in the circulating blood by way of the warmth-organism—works as the spiritual entity which, as it were, sends down the will out of the warmth, via the air, into the fluid organism. Thus everything in the human organism works upon everything else. But we get nowhere if we have only general, abstract ideas of this interpenetration; we reach a result only if we can evolve a concrete idea of the constitution of man and of how everything that is around him participates in his make-up.

The condition of sleep, too, can be understood only if we go much more closely into these matters. During sleep it is only the physical body and the etheric body that remain as they are during the waking state; the Ego and the astral body are outside. But in the sleeping human being the forces that are within the physical and etheric bodies can also be active—on the aeriform organism and the warmth-organism as well.

When we turn to consider waking life, from what has been said we shall understand the connection of the Ego with the astral body and with the whole organism. During sleep, when the Ego and the astral body are outside, the four elements are nevertheless within the human organism: the solid supporting structure, the fluid organism, but also the air organism in which the astral body otherwise works, and the warmth-organism in which the Ego otherwise works. These elements are within the human organism and they work in just as regularly organized a way during sleep as during the waking state, when the Ego and the astral body are active within them.

During the sleeping state we have within us, instead of the Ego—which is now outside—the spirit which pervades the cosmos and which in waking life we have driven out through our Ego which is part of that spirit. During sleep our warmth-body is pervaded by cosmic spirituality, our air organism by what may be called cosmic astrality (or world-soul), which we also drive out while we are awake.

Waking life and sleeping life may therefore also be studied from this point of view. When we are asleep our warmth-organism is permeated by the cosmic spirituality which on waking we drive out through our Ego, for in waking life it is the Ego that brings about in the warmth-organism what is otherwise brought about by the cosmic spirituality. It is the same with the cosmic astrality; we drive it out when we wake up and readmit it into our organism when we fall asleep. Thus we can say: In that we

19

leave our body during sleep, we allow the cosmic spirit to draw into our warmth-organism, and the world-soul, or the cosmic astrality, into our aeriform organism.

If we study man without preconceived ideas, we acquire understanding not only of his relation to the surrounding physical world, but also of his relation to the cosmic spirituality and to the cosmic astrality.

This is one aspect of the subject. We can now consider it also from the aspect of knowledge, of cognition, and you will see how the two aspects tally with each other. It is customary to call 'knowledge' only what man experiences through perception and the intellectual elaboration of perceptions from the moment of waking to that of falling asleep. But thereby we come to know man's physical environment only. If we adhere to the principles of spiritual-scientific thinking and do not indulge in fantasy, we shall not, of course, regard the pictures of dream-life as immediate realities in themselves, neither shall we seek in dreams for knowledge as we seek it in waking mental activity and perception. Nevertheless at a certain lower level, dreaming is a form of knowledge. It is a particular form of physical self-knowledge. Roughly, it can be obvious that a man has been 'dreaming' inner conditions when, let us say, he wakes up with the dream of having endured the heat of an intensely hot stove and then, on waking, finds that he is feverish or is suffering from some kind of inflammatory condition. In other ways too, dreams assume definite configuration. A man may dream of coiling snakes when something is out of order in the intestines; or he may dream of caves into which he is obliged to creep, and then wake up with a headache, and so on. Obscurely and dimly, dreams point to man's inner organic life, and we can certainly speak of a kind of lower knowledge as being present in dreams. There is merely an enhancement of this when the dreams of particularly sensitive people present very exact reflections of the organism.

It is generally believed that deep, dreamless sleep contributes nothing at all in the way of knowledge, that dreamless sleep is quite worthless as far as knowledge is concerned. But this is not the case. Dreamless sleep has its definite task to perform for knowledge—knowledge that has an individual-personal bearing. If we did not sleep, if our life were not continually interrupted by periods of sleep, we should be incapable of reaching a clear concept of the 'I,' the Ego; we could have no clear realization of our identity. We should experience nothing except the world outside and lose ourselves entirely in it. Insufficient attention is paid to this, because people are not in the habit of thinking in a really unprejudiced way about what is experienced in the life of soul and in the bodily life.

We look back over our life, at the series of pictures of our experiences to the point to which memory extends. But this whole stream of remembrances is interrupted every night by sleep. In the backward survey of our life the intervals of sleep are ignored. It does not occur to us that the stream of memories is ever and again interrupted by periods of sleep. The fact that it is so interrupted means that, without being conscious of it, we look into a void, a nothingness, as well as into a sphere that is filled with content. If here we have a white sphere with a black area in the middle, we see the white and in the middle the black, which, compared with the white, is a void, a nothingness. (This is not absolutely accurate but we need not think of that at the moment.) We see the black area, we see that in the white sphere something has been left free, but this is equally a positive im-

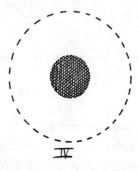

IV

pression although not identical with the impressions of the white sphere. The black area also gives a positive impression. In the same way the experience is a positive one when we are looking back over our life and nothing flows into this retrospective survey from the periods of sleep. What we slept through is actually included in the retrospective survey, although we are not directly conscious of it because consciousness is focussed entirely on the pictures left by waking life. But this consciousness is inwardly strengthened through the fact that in the field of retrospective vision there are also empty places; this constitutes the source of our consciousness in so far as it is inward consciousness. We should lose ourselves entirely in the external world if we were always awake, if this waking state were not continually interrupted by sleep. But whereas dream-filled sleep mirrors back to us in chaotic pictures certain fragments of our inner, organic conditions, dreamless sleep imparts to us the consciousness of our organization as man—again, therefore, knowledge. Through waking consciousness we perceive the external world. Through dreams we perceive—but dimly and without firm definition—single fragments of our inner, organic conditions. Through dreamless sleep we come to know our organization in its totality, although dimly and obscurely. Thus we have already considered three stages of knowledge: dreamless sleep, dream-filled sleep, the waking state.

Then we come to the three higher forms of knowledge: Imagination, Inspiration, Intuition. These are the stages which lie *above* the waking consciousness and as states of consciousness become ever clearer, yielding more and more data of knowledge; whereas *below* the ordinary consciousness we come to those chaotic fragments of knowledge which are nevertheless necessary for ordinary forms of experience.

This is how we must think of the field of consciousness. We should not speak of having only the ordinary waking consciousness any more than we should speak of having only the familiar solid organism. We must speak to the effect that the solid organism is something that exists within a clearly demarcated space, so that if we think in an entirely materialistic way, we shall take this to be the human organism itself. We must remember that ordinary consciousness is actually present, that its ideas and mental pictures come to us in definite outlines. But we should neither think that we have the solid body only, nor that we have this day-consciousness only. For the solid body is permeated by the fluid body which has an inwardly fluctuating organization, and again the clear day-consciousness is permeated by the dream-consciousness, yielding pictures which have no sharp outlines but fluctuating outlines, for consciousness here itself becomes 'fluid' in a certain sense. And as well as the fluid organism we have the air organism, which during the sleeping state is sustained by something that is not ourselves, and hence is not entirely, but only partially and transiently, connected with our own life of soul—namely in waking life only; nevertheless we have it within us as an actual organism.

We have also a third state of consciousness, the dark consciousness of dreamless sleep, in which ideas and thought-pictures become not only hazy but dulled to the degree of inner darkness; in dreamless sleep we cease altogether to experience consciousness itself, just as under certain circumstances, while we are asleep, we cease to experience the aeriform body.

warmth body	ego
air body	dream consciousness
fluid body	sleep consciousness
solid body	

V

So you see, no matter whether we study man from the inner or the outer aspect, we reach an ever fuller and wider conception of his being and constitution. Passing from the solid body to the fluid body to the air body to the warmth body, we come to the life of *soul*. Passing from the clear day-consciousness to the dream-consciousness, we come to the *body*. And we come to the body in a still deeper sense through the knowledge of being within it through dreamless sleep. When we carry the waking consciousness right down into the consciousness of dreamless sleep and observe the human being in the members of his consciousness, we come to the bodily constitution of man. When we consider the bodily constitution itself, from its solid state up to its warmth-state, we pass out of the bodily constitution.

This shows you how necessary it is not simply to accept what is presented to biased, external observation. There, on the one side, is the solid body, to which materialistic-mechanistic thought is anchored; and on the other side there is the life of soul which to modern consciousness appears endowed with content only in the form of experiences belonging to the clear day-consciousness. Thought based on external observation alone does not go downwards from this state of consciousness. (See diagram I: Ego), for if it did it would come to the body. It does not go downwards from the spiritual body (warmth-body), for if it did it would be led to the solid body. This kind of thinking studies the solid body without either the fluid body, the air body or the warmth-body, and the day-consciousness without that which in reality reflects the inner bodily nature— without the dream-consciousness and the consciousness of dreamless sleep.

On the basis of academic psychology, the question is asked: How does the soul-and-spirit live in the physical man?—In reality we have the solid body, the fluid body, the air body and the warmth-body. (Diagram V.) By way of the warmth-body the Ego unfolds the clear day-consciousness. But coming downwards we have the dream-consciousness, and still farther downwards the consciousness of dreamless sleep. Descending even farther (diagram V, horizontal shading), we come—as you know from the book *Occult Science*—to still another state of consciousness which we need not consider now. If we ask how what is here on the right (diagram V) is related to what is on the left, we shall find that they harmonize, for *here* (arrow at left side), ascending from below upwards, we come to the soul-realm; and *here* (arrow at right side) we come to the bodily constitution: the right and the left harmonize.

But fundamentally speaking, the externalized thinking of today takes account only of the solid body, and again only of *this* state of consciousness (Ego). The Ego hovers in the clouds and the solid body stands on the ground—and no relation is found between the two. If you read the literature of modern psychology you will find the most incredible hypotheses of how the soul works upon the body. But this is all due to the fact that only one *part* of the

warmth body	ego soul realm
air body	dream consciousness
fluid body	sleep consciousness
solid body	

VI

body is taken into account, and then something that is entirely separated from it—one *part* of the soul. (Diagram VI, oblique shading.)

That Spiritual Science aims everywhere for wholeness of view, that it must in very truth build the bridge between the bodily constitution on the one side and the life of soul on the other, that it draws attention to states of being where the soul-element becomes a bodily element, the bodily element a soul-element—all this riles our contemporaries, who insist upon not going beyond what presents itself to external, prejudiced contemplation.

Ego—Will—Warmth-Organism—Warmth Ether.
Astral body—Feeling—Air Organism—Light Ether.
Etheric body—Thinking—Fluid Organism—Chemical Ether.

II

The Moral as the Source of World Creative Power

I TRIED yesterday to give certain indications about the constitution of man, and at the end it was possible to show that a really penetrating study of human nature is able to build a bridge between man's external constitution and what he unfolds, through self-consciousness, in his inner life. As a rule no such bridge is built, or only very inadequately built, particularly in the science current today. It became clear to us that in order to build this bridge we must know how man's constitution is properly to be regarded. We saw that the solid or solid-fluid organism—which is the sole object of study today and is alone recognized by modern science as organic in the real sense—we saw that this must be regarded as only one of the organisms in man's constitution; that the existence of a fluid organism, an aeriform organism, and a warmth-organism must also be recognized. This makes it possible for us also to perceive how those members of man's nature which we are accustomed to regard as such, penetrate into this delicately organized constitution. Naturally, up to the warmth-organism itself, everything is to be conceived as physical body. But it is paramountly the etheric body that takes hold of the fluid body, of everything that is fluid in the human organism; in everything aeriform, the astral body is paramountly active, and in the warmth-organism, the Ego. By recognizing this we can as it were remain in the physical but at the same time reach up to the spiritual.

We also studied consciousness at the different levels. As I said yesterday, it is usual to take account only of the consciousness known to us in waking life from the moment of waking to the moment of falling asleep. We perceive the objects around us, reason about these perceptions with our intellect; we also have feelings in connection with these perceptions, and we have our will-impulses. But we experience this whole nexus of consciousness as something which, in its qualities, differs completely from the physical which alone is taken account of by ordinary science. It is not possible, without further ado, to build a bridge from these imponderable, incorporeal experiences in the domain of consciousness to the other objects of perception studied in physiology or physical anatomy. But in regard to consciousness too, we know from ordinary life that in addition to the waking consciousness, there is dream-consciousness, and we heard yesterday that dreams are essentially pictures or symbols of inner organic processes. Something is going on within us all the time, and in our dreams it comes to expression in pictures. I said that we may dream of coiling snakes when we have some intestinal disorder, or we may dream of an excessively hot stove and wake up with palpitations of the heart. The over-heated stove symbolized irregular beating of the heart, the snakes symbolized the intestines, and so forth. Dreams point us to our organism; the consciousness of dreamless sleep is, as it were, an experience of nullity, of the void. But I explained that this experience of the void is necessary in order that man shall feel himself connected with his bodily nature. As an Ego he would feel no connection with his body if he did not leave it during sleep and seek for it again on waking. It is through the deprivation undergone between falling asleep and waking that he is able to feel·himself united with the body. So from the ordinary consciousness which has really nothing to do with our own essential being beyond the fact that it enables us to have perceptions and ideas, we are led to the dream-consciousness which has to do with actual bodily processes. We are therefore led to the body. And we are led to the body even more strongly when we pass into the consciousness of dreamless sleep. Thus we can say: On the one hand our conception of the life of soul is such that it leads us to the body. And our conception of the bodily constitution, comprising as it does the fluid organism, the aeriform organism, the warmth-organism and thus becoming by degrees more rarefied, leads us to the realm of soul. It is absolutely necessary to take these things into consideration if we are to reach a view of the world that can really satisfy us.

The great question with which we have been concerning ourselves for weeks, the cardinal question in man's conception of the world, is this: How is the moral world-order connected with the physical world-order? As has been said so often, the prevailing world-view—which relies entirely upon natural science for knowledge of the outer physical world and can only resort to earlier religious beliefs when it is a matter of any really comprehensive understanding of the life of soul, for in modern psychology there is no longer any such understanding—this world-view is unable to build a bridge. There, on the one side, is the physical world. According to the modern world-view, this is a conglomeration from a primeval nebula, and everything will eventually become a kind of slag-heap in the universe. This is the picture of the evolutionary process presented to us by the science of today, and it is the one and only picture in which a really honest modern scientist can find reality.

Within this picture a moral world-order has no place. It is there on its own. Man receives the moral impulses into himself as impulses of soul. But if the assertions of natural science are true, everything that is astir with life, and finally man himself, came out of the primeval nebula and the moral ideals well up in him. And when, as is alleged, the world becomes a slag-heap, this will also be the graveyard of all moral ideals. They will have vanished.—No bridge can possibly be built, and what is worse, modern science cannot, without being inconsistent, admit the existence of morality in the world-order. Only if modern science is inconsistent can it accept the moral world-order as valid. It cannot do so if it is consistent. The root of all this is that the only kind of anatomy in existence is concerned exclusively with the solid organism, and no account is taken of the fact that man also has within him a fluid organism, an aeriform organism, and a warmth-organism. If you picture to yourselves that as well as the solid organism with its configuration into bones, muscles, nerve-fibres and so forth, you also have a fluid organism and an aeriform organism—though these are of course fluctuating and

31

inwardly mobile—and a warmth-organism, if you picture this you will more easily understand what I shall now have to say on the basis of spiritual-scientific observation.

Think of a man whose very soul is fired with enthusiasm for a high moral ideal, for the ideal of generosity, of freedom, of goodness, of love, or whatever it may be. He may also feel enthusiasm for examples of the practical expression of these ideals. But nobody can conceive that the enthusiasm which fires the soul penetrates into the bones and muscles as described by modern physiology or anatomy. If you really take counsel with yourself, however, you will find it quite possible to conceive that when a man has enthusiasm for a high moral ideal, this enthusiasm has an effect upon the warmth-organism.—There, you see, we have come from the realm of soul into the physical!

Taking this as an example, we may say: Moral ideals come to expression in an enhancement of warmth in the warmth-organism. Not only is man warmed in soul through what he experiences in the way of moral ideals, but he becomes organically warmer as well—though this is not so easy to prove with physical instruments. Moral ideals, then, have a stimulating, invigorating effect upon the warmth-organism.

You must think of this as a real and concrete happening: enthusiasm for a moral ideal—stimulation of the warmth-organism. There is more vigorous activity in the warmth-organism when the soul is fired by a moral ideal. Neither does this remain without effect upon the rest of man's constitution. As well as the warmth-organism he also has the air-organism. He inhales and exhales the air; but during the inbreathing and outbreathing process the air is within him. It is of course inwardly in movement, in fluctuation, but equally with the warmth-organism it is an actual air-organism in man. Warmth, quickened by a moral ideal, works in turn upon the air-organism, because warmth pervades the whole human organism, pervades every part of it. The effect upon the air-organism is not that of warming only, for when the warmth, stimulated in the warmth-organism, works upon the air-organism, it imparts to it something that I can only call a *source of light*. Sources of light, as it were, are imparted to the air-organism, so that moral ideals which have a stimulating effect upon the warmth-organism produce sources of light in the air-organism. To external perception and for ordinary consciousness these sources of light are not in themselves luminous, but they manifest in man's astral body. To begin with, they are curbed—if I may use this expression— through the air that is within man. They are, so to speak, still dark light, in the sense that the seed of a plant is not yet the developed plant. Nevertheless man has a source of light within him through the fact that he can be fired with enthusiasm for moral ideals, for moral impulses.

We also have within us the fluid organism. Warmth, stimulated in the warmth-organism by moral ideals, produces in the air-organism what may be called a source of light which remains, to begin with, curbed and hidden. Within the fluid organism— because everything in man's constitution interpenetrates—a process takes place which I said yesterday actually underlies the outer tone conveyed in the air. I said that the air is only the body of the tone, and

33

anyone who regards the essential reality of tone as a matter of vibrations of the air, speaks of tones just as he would speak of man as having nothing except the outwardly visible physical body. The air with its vibrating waves is nothing but the outer body of the tone. In the human being this tone, this *spiritual* tone, is not produced in the air-organism through the moral ideal, but in the fluid organism. The sources of tone, therefore, arise in the fluid organism.

We regard the solid organism as the densest of all, as the one that supports and bears all the others. Within it, too, something is produced as in the case of the other organisms. In the solid organism there is produced what we call a *seed of life*—but it is an *etheric*, not a physical seed of life such as issues from the female organism at a birth. This etheric seed which lies in the deepest levels of subconsciousness is actually the primal source of tone and, in a certain sense, even the source of light. This is entirely hidden from ordinary consciousness, but it is there within the human being.

Think of all the experiences in your life that came from aspiration for moral ideas—be it that they attracted you merely as ideas, or that you saw them coming to expression in others, or that you felt inwardly satisfied by having put such impulses into practice, by letting your deeds be fired by moral ideals . . . all this goes down into the air-organism as a source of *light*, into the fluid organism as a source of *tone*, into the solid organism as a source of *life*.

These processes are withdrawn from the field of man's consciousness but they operate within him nevertheless. They become free when he lays aside his physical body at death. What is thus produced in us through moral ideals, or through the loftiest and purest ideas, does not bear immediate fruit. For during the life between birth and death, moral ideas as such become fruitful only in so far as we remain in the life of ideas, and in so far as we feel a certain satisfaction in moral deeds performed. But this is merely a matter of remembrance, and has nothing to do with what actually penetrates down into the different organisms as the result of enthusiasm for moral ideals.

So we see that our whole constitution, beginning with the warmth-organism, is, in very fact, permeated by moral ideals. And when at death the etheric body, the astral body, and the Ego emerge from the physical body, these higher members of our human nature are filled with all the impressions we have had. Our Ego was living in the warmth-organism, when it was quickened by moral ideas. We were living in our air-organism, into which were implanted sources of *light* which now, after death, go forth into the cosmos together with us. In our fluid organism, *tone* was kindled which now becomes part of the Music of the Spheres, resounding from us into the cosmos. And we bring *life* with us when we pass out into the cosmos through the portal of death.

You will now begin to have an inkling of what the life that pervades the universe really is. Where are the sources of life? They lie in that which quickens those moral ideals which fire man with enthusiasm. We come to the point of saying to ourselves that if today we allow ourselves to be inspired by moral ideals, these will carry forth life, tone and light into the universe and will become *world-creative*. We carry out into the universe world-creative power, and the source of this power is the moral element.

So when we study the · *vhole* man we find a bridge between moral ideals and what works as life-giving force in the physical world, even in the chemical sense. For tone works in the chemical sense by assembling substances and dispersing them again. Light in the world has its source in the moral stimuli, in the warmth-organisms of men. Thus we look into the future—new worlds take shape. And as in the case of the plant we must go back to the seed, so in the case of these future worlds that will come into being, we must go back to the seeds which lie in us as moral ideals.

And now think of theoretical ideas in contrast to moral ideals. In the case of theoretical ideas, everything is different, no matter how significant these ideas may be, for theoretical ideas produce the very opposite effect to that of stimulus. They *cool down* the warmth-organism—that is the difference.

Moral ideas, or ideas of a moral-religious character, which fire us with enthusiasm and become impulses for deeds, work as world-creative powers. Theoretical ideas and speculations have a cooling, subduing effect upon the warmth-organism. Because this is so, they also have a *paralyzing* effect upon the air-organism and upon the source of light within it; they have a *deadening* effect upon tone, and an *extinguishing* effect upon life. In our theoretical ideas the creations of the pre-existing world come to their end. When we formulate theoretical ideas a universe dies in them. Thus do we bear within us the death of a universe and the dawn of a universe.

Here we come to the point where he who is initiated into the secrets of the universe cannot speak as so many speak today, of the conservation of energy or the conservation of matter. It is simply not true that matter is conserved forever. Matter dies to the point of nullity, to zero-point. In our own organism, energy dies to the point of nullity through the fact that we formulate theoretical thoughts. But if we did not do so, if the universe did not continually die in us, we should not be man in the true sense. Because the universe dies in us, we are endowed with self-consciousness and are able to think about the universe. But these thoughts are the corpse of the universe. We become conscious of the universe as a corpse only, and it is this that makes us Man.

A past world dies within us, down to its very matter and energy. It is only because a new universe at once begins to dawn that we do not notice this dying of matter and its immediate rebirth. Through man's theoretical thinking, matter—substantiality—is brought to its end; through his *moral* thinking, matter and cosmic energy are imbued with new life. Thus what goes on inside the boundary of the human skin is connected with the dying and birth of worlds. This is how the moral order and the natural order are connected. The natural world dies away in man; in the realm of the moral a new natural world comes to birth.

Moral Ideals
    stimulate the warmth-organism.
    producing in the air-organism—sources of *Light*.

producing in the fluid organism—sources of *Tone*.
producing in the solid organism—seeds of *Life*.
(etheric).

Theoretical thoughts
cool down the warmth organism.
paralyze the sources of Light.
deaden the sources of Tone.
extinguish Life.

Because of unwillingness to consider these things, the ideas of the imperishability of matter and energy were invented. If energy were imperishable and matter were imperishable there would be no moral world-order. But today it is desired to keep this truth concealed and modern thought has every reason to do so, because otherwise it would have to eliminate the moral world-order—which in actual fact it does by speaking of the law of the conservation of matter and energy. If matter is conserved, or energy is conserved, the moral world-order is nothing but an illusion, a mirage. We can understand the course of the world's development only if we grasp how out of this 'illusory' moral world-order—for so it is when it is grasped in thoughts—new worlds come into being.

Nothing of this can be grasped if we study only the solid component of man's constitution. To understand it we must pass from the solid organism through the fluid and aeriform organisms to the warmth-organism. Man's connection with the universe can be understood only if the physical is traced upwards to that rarefied state wherein the soul can be directly active in the rarefied physical element, as for example in warmth. Then it is possible to find the connection between body and soul.

However many treatises on psychology may be written—if they are based upon what is studied today in anatomy and physiology it will not be possible to find any transition to the life of soul from this solid, or solid-fluid bodily constitution. The life of soul will not be revealed as such. But if the bodily substance is traced back to warmth, a bridge can be built from what exists in the body as warmth to what works from out of the soul into the warmth in the human organism. There is warmth both without and within the human organism. As we have heard, in man's constitution warmth is an organism; the soul, the soul-and-spirit, takes hold of this warmth-organism and by way of the warmth all that becomes active which we inwardly experience as the moral. By the 'moral' I do not of course mean what philistines mean by it, but I mean the moral in its totality, that is to say, all those impulses that come to us, for example when we contemplate the majesty of the universe, when we say to ourselves: We are born out of the cosmos and we are responsible for what goes on in the world.—I mean the impulses that come to us when the knowledge yielded by Spiritual Science inspires us to work for the sake of the future. When we regard Spiritual Science itself as a source of the moral, this, more than anything else, can fill us with enthusiasm for the moral, and this enthusiasm, born of spiritual-scientific knowledge, becomes in itself a source of morality in the higher sense. But what is generally called 'moral' represents no more than a subordinate sphere of the moral in the universal sense.

—All the ideas we evolve about the external world, about Nature in her finished array, are theoretical ideas. No matter with what exactitude we envisage a machine in terms of mathematics and the principles of mechanics, or the universe in the sense of the Copernican system—this is nothing but theoretical thinking, and the ideas thus formulated constitute a force of death within us; a corpse of the universe is within us in the form of thoughts, of ideas.

These matters create deeper and deeper insight into the universe in its totality. There are not two orders, a natural order and a moral order in juxtaposition, but the two are one. This is a truth that must be realized by the man of today. Otherwise he must ever and again be asking himself: How can my moral impulses take effect in a world in which a natural order alone prevails?—This indeed was the terrible problem that weighed upon men in the nineteenth century and early twentieth century: How is it possible to conceive of any transition from the natural world into the moral world, from the moral world into the natural world?—The fact is that nothing can help to solve this perplexing, fateful problem except spiritual-scientific insight into Nature on the one side and Spirit on the other.

With the premises yielded by this knowledge we shall also be able to get to the root of something that is presented as a branch of science today and has already penetrated into the general consciousness of men. Our world-view today is based upon Copernicanism. Until the year 1827 the Copernican conception of the universe which was elaborated by Kepler and then diluted into theory by Newton, was tabooed by the Roman Catholic Church. No orthodox

Catholic was allowed to believe it. Since that year the prohibition has been lifted; and the Copernican view of the universe has taken root so strongly in the general consciousness that anyone who does not base his own world-view upon it is regarded as a fool.

What *is* this Copernican picture of the universe? —It is in reality a picture built up purely on the basis of mathematical principles, mathematical-mechanical principles. The rudiments of it began, very gradually, to be unfolded in Greece,* where, however, echoes of earlier thought—for example in the Ptolemaic view of the universe—still persisted. And in course of time this developed into the Copernican system that is taught nowadays to every child.

We can look back from this world-conception to ancient times when man's picture of the universe was very different. All that has remained of it are those traditions which in the form in which they exist today—in astrology and the like—are sheer dilettantism. That is what has remained of ancient astronomy, and it has also remained, ossified and paralyzed, in the symbols of certain secret societies, Masonic societies and the like. There is usually entire ignorance of the fact that these things are relics of an ancient astronomy. This ancient astronomy was quite different from that of today, for it was based, not upon mathematical principles but upon ancient clairvoyant vision.

Entirely false ideas prevail today of how an earlier humanity acquired its astronomical-astrological knowledge. This was acquired through an instinctive-clairvoyant vision of the universe. The earliest Post-

* Particularly by Aristarchos of Samos, the Greek astronomer, circa 250 B.C.

Atlantean peoples saw the heavenly bodies as spirit-forms, spirit-entities, whereas man today regards them merely as physical structures. When the ancient peoples spoke of the celestial bodies, of the planets or of the fixed stars, they were speaking of *spiritual beings*. Today, the sun is pictured as a globe of burning gas which radiates light into the universe. But for the men of ancient times the sun was a living Being and they regarded the sun which their eyes beheld simply as the outward manifestation of this Spirit-Being at the place where the sun stands in the universe; and it was the same in regard to the other heavenly bodies—they were seen as Spirit-Beings. We must think of an age which came to an end long before the time of the Mystery of Golgotha, when the sun out yonder in the universe and everything in the stars was conceived of as living spirit-reality, living Being. Then came an intermediary period when men no longer had this vision, when they regarded the planets, at any rate, as physical, but still thought of them as pervaded by living souls. In times when it was no longer known how the physical passes over by stages into what is of the soul, how what is of the soul passes over by stages into the physical, how in reality the two are united, men postulated physical existence on the one side and soul-existence on the other. They thought of the correspondences between these two realms just as most psychologists today—if they admit the existence of a soul at all—still think, namely that the soul and the physical nature of man are identical. This, of course, leads thought to absurdity; or there is the so-called 'psycho-physical parallelism,' which again is nothing else than a stupid way of formulating something that is not understood.

Then came the age when the heavenly bodies were regarded as physical structures, circling or stationary, attracting or repelling one another in accordance with mathematical laws. To be sure, in every epoch there existed a knowledge—in earlier times a more instinctive knowledge—of how things are in reality. But in the present age this instinctive knowledge no longer suffices; what in earlier times was known instinctively must now be acquired by *conscious effort*. And if we enquire how those who were able to view the universe in its totality—that is to say, in its physical, psychical and spiritual aspects—if we enquire how these men pictured the sun, we must say: They pictured it first and foremost as a Spirit-Being. Those who were initiated conceived of this Spirit-Being as the source of the moral. In my *Philosophy of Spiritual Activity* I have said that 'moral intuitions' are drawn from this source—but drawn from it in the earthly world, for the moral intuitions shine forth from *man*, from what can live in him as enthusiasm for the moral.

Think of how greatly our responsibility is increased when we realize: If here on the earth there were no soul capable of being fired with enthusiasm for true and genuine morality, for the spiritual moral order in general, nothing could be contributed towards the progress of our world, towards a new creation; our world would be led towards its death.

This force of light that is on the earth (diagram VII) rays out into the universe. This is, to begin with, imperceptible to ordinary vision; we do not perceive how the moral impulses in man ray out from the earth into the universe. If a grievous age were to dawn over the earth, an age when millions and millions of men would perish through lack of spirituality—

43

spirituality conceived of here as including the moral, which indeed it does—if there were only a dozen men filled with moral enthusiasm, the earth would *still*

VII

ray out a spiritual, sun-like force! This force rays out only to a certain distance. At this point it mirrors itself, as it were, in itself, so that here (diagram VIII)

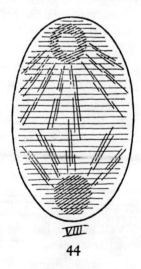

VIII

there arises the reflection of what radiates from *man*. And in every epoch the initiates regarded this reflection as the sun. For as I have so often said, there is nothing physical here. Where ordinary astronomy speaks of the existence of an incandescent globe of gas, there is merely the reflection of a spiritual reality in physical appearance.

You see, therefore, how great is the distance separating the Copernican view of the world, and even the old astrology, from what was the inmost secret of Initiation. The best illustration of these things is provided by the fact that in an epoch when great power was vested in the hands of groups of men, who, as they declared, considered that such truths were dangerous for the masses and did not wish them to be communicated, one who was an idealist—the Emperor Julian (called for this reason 'the Apostate') —wanted to impart these truths to the world and was then brought to his death by cunning means. There are reasons which induce certain occult societies to withhold vital secrets of world-existence, because by so doing they are able to wield a certain power. If in the days of the Emperor Julian certain occult societies guarded their secrets so strictly that they acquiesced in his murder, it need not surprise us if those who are the custodians of certain secrets today do not reveal them but want to withhold them from the masses in order to enhance their power—it need not surprise us if such people hate to realize that at least the beginnings of such secrets are being unveiled. And now you will understand some of the deeper reasons for the bitter hatred that is levelled against Spiritual Science, against what Spiritual Science feels it a duty to bring to mankind at the present time.

But we are living in an age when either earthly civilization will be doomed to perish, or certain secrets will be restored to mankind—truths which hitherto have in a certain way been guarded as secrets, which were once revealed to men through instinctive clairvoyance but must now be reacquired by fully conscious vision, not only of the physical but also of the spiritual that is within the physical.

What was the real aim of Julian the Apostate?—He wished to make clear to the people: 'You are becoming more and more accustomed to look only at the physical sun; but there is a spiritual Sun of which the physical sun is only the mirror-image!' In his own way he wished to communicate the Christ-Secret to the world. But in our age it is desired that the connection of Christ, the spiritual Sun, with the physical sun, shall be kept hidden. That is why certain authorities rage most violently of all when we speak of the Christ Mystery in connection with the Sun Mystery. All kinds of calumnies are then spread abroad.—But Spiritual Science is assuredly a matter of importance in the present age, and those alone who regard it as such view it with the earnestness that is its due.

III

The Path to Freedom and Love and Their Significance in World Events

MAN STANDS in the world as a thinking, contemplative, being on the one hand, and as a doer, a being of action, on the other; with his feeling he lives within both these spheres. With his feeling he responds, on the one side, to what is presented to his observation; on the other side, feeling enters into his actions, his deeds. We need only consider how a man may be satisfied or dissatisfied with the success or lack of success of his deeds, how in truth all action is accompanied by impulses of feeling, and we shall see that, in reality, feeling links the two poles of our being: the pole of thinking and the pole of deed, of action. Only through the fact that we are thinking beings are we *Man* in the truest sense. Consider too, how everything that gives us the consciousness of our essential manhood is connected with the fact that we can inwardly picture the world around us; we live in this world and can contemplate it. To imagine that we cannot contemplate the world would entail forfeiting our essential manhood. As doers, as men of action, we have our place in the social life and fundamentally speaking, everything we accomplish between birth and death has a certain significance in this social life.

In so far as we are contemplative beings, *thought* operates in us; in so far as we are doers, that is to say, social beings, *will* operates in us. It is not the case in human nature, nor is it ever so, that things can simply be thought of intellectually side by side with one another; the truth is that whatever is an active factor in life can be characterized from one aspect or another; the forces of the world interpenetrate, flow into each other. Mentally, we can picture ourselves as beings of thought, also as beings of will. But even when we are entirely engrossed in contemplation, when the outer world is completely stilled, the will is continually active. And again, when we are performing deeds, thought is active in us. It is inconceivable that anything should proceed from us in the way of actions or deeds—which may also take effect in the realm of social life—without our identifying ourselves in thought with what thus takes place. In everything that is of the nature of will, the element of thought is contained; and in everything that is of the nature of thought, will is present. It is essential to be quite clear about what is involved here if we seriously want to build the bridge between the moral-spiritual world-order and natural-physical world-order.

Imagine that you are living for a time purely in reflection as usually understood, that you are engaging in no kind of outward activity at all, but are wholly engrossed in thought. You must realize, however, that in this life of thought, *will* is also active; will is then at work in your inner being, raying out its forces into the realm of thought. When we picture the

48

thinking human being in this way, when we realize that the will is radiating all the time into his thoughts, something will certainly strike us concerning life and its realities. If we review all the thoughts we have formulated, we shall find in every case that they are linked with something in our environment, something that we ourselves have experienced. Between birth and death we have, in a certain respect, no thoughts other than those brought to us by life. If our life has been rich in experiences we have a rich thought-content; if our experiences have been meagre, we have a meagre thought-content. The thought-content represents our inner destiny—to a certain extent. But within this life of thought there is something that is inherently our own; what is inherently our own is *how* we connect thoughts with one another and dissociate them again, *how* we elaborate them inwardly, *how* we arrive at judgments and draw conclusions, *how* we orientate ourselves in the life of thought—all this is inherently our own. The will in our life of thought is our own.

If we study this life of thought in careful self-examination, we shall certainly realize that thoughts, as far as their actual content is concerned, come to us from outside, but that it is we ourselves who elaborate these thoughts.—Fundamentally speaking, therefore, in respect of our world of thought we are entirely dependent upon the experiences brought to us by our birth, by our destiny. But through the will which rays out from the depths of the soul, we carry into what thus comes to us from the outer world, something that is inherently our own. For the fulfilment of what self-knowledge demands of us it is highly important to keep separate in our minds how, on the one side, the thought-content comes to us from the surrounding world and how, on the other, the force of the will, coming from within our being, rays into the world of thought.

How, in reality, do we become inwardly more and more spiritual?—Not by taking in as many thoughts as possible from the surrounding world, for these thoughts merely reproduce in pictures this outer world, which is a physical, material world. Constantly to be running in pursuit of sensations does not make us more spiritual. We become more spiritual through the inner, will-permeated work we carry out in our thoughts. This is why meditation, too, consists in not indulging in haphazard thoughts but in holding certain easily envisaged thoughts in the very centre of our consciousness, drawing them there with a strong effort of will. And the greater the strength and intensity of this inner radiation of will into the sphere of thinking, the more spiritual we become. When we take in thoughts from the outer material world—and between birth and death we can take in only such thoughts— we become, as you can easily realize, unfree; for we are given over to the concatenations of things and events in the external world; as far as the actual content of the thoughts is concerned, we are obliged to think as the external world prescribes; only when we elaborate the thoughts do we become free in the real sense.

Now it is possible to attain complete freedom in our inner life if we increasingly efface and exclude the actual thought-content, in so far as this comes from outside, and kindle into greater activity the element of will which streams through our thoughts when we form judgments, draw conclusions and the like. Thereby, however, our thinking becomes what I have called in my *Philosophy of Spiritual Activity: pure* thinking. We think, but in our thinking there is nothing but will. I have laid particular emphasis on this in the new edition of the book (1918). What is thus within us lies in the sphere of thinking. But pure thinking may equally be called pure *will*. Thus from the realm of thinking we reach the realm of will, when we become inwardly free; our thinking attains such maturity that it is entirely irradiated by will; it no longer takes anything in from outside, but its very life is of the nature of will. By progressively strengthening the impulse of will in our thinking we prepare ourselves for what I have called in the *Philosophy of Spiritual Activity*, "Moral Imagination." Moral Imagination rises to the Moral Intuitions which then pervade and illuminate our will that has now become thought, or our thinking that has now become will. In this way we raise ourselves above the sway of the 'necessity' prevailing in the material world, permeate ourselves with the force that is inherently our own, and prepare for Moral Intuition. And everything that can stream into man from the spiritual world has its foundation, primarily, in these Moral Intuitions. Therefore *freedom* dawns when we enable the will to become an ever mightier and mightier force in our thinking.

Now let us consider the human being from the opposite pole, that of the will. When does the will present itself with particular clarity through what we do?—Now when we sneeze, let us say, we are also doing something, but we cannot, surely, ascribe to ourselves any definite impulse of will when we sneeze! When we speak, we are doing something in which will is undoubtedly contained. But think how, in speaking, deliberate intent and absence of intent, volition and absence of volition, intermingle. You have to *learn* to speak, and in such a way that you are no longer obliged to formulate each single word by dint of an effort of will; an element of instinct enters into speech. In ordinary life at least, it is so, and it is emphatically so in the case of those who do not strive for spirituality. Garrulous people who are always opening their mouths in order to say something or other in which very little thought is contained give others an opportunity of noticing—they themselves, of course, do *not* notice—how much there is in speech that is instinctive and involuntary. But the more we go out beyond our organic life and pass over to activity that is liberated, as it were, from organic processes, the more do we carry thoughts into our actions and deeds. Sneezing is still entirely a matter of organic life; speaking is largely connected with organic life; walking really very little; what we do with the hands, also very little. And so we come by degrees to actions which are more and more emancipated from our organic life. We accompany such actions with our thoughts, although we do not know how the will streams into these thoughts. If we are not somnambulists and do not go about in this condition, our actions will always be accompanied by our thoughts. We carry our thoughts into our actions, and the more our actions evolve towards perfection, the more are our thoughts being carried into them.

Our inner life is constantly deepened when we send will—our own inherent force—into our thinking, when we permeate our thinking with will. We bring will into thinking and thereby attain freedom. As we

52

gradually perfect our actions we finally succeed in sending thoughts into these actions; we irradiate our actions—which proceed from our will—with thoughts. On the one side (inwards) we live a life of thought; we permeate this with the will and thus find freedom. On the other side (outwards) our actions stream forth from our will, and we permeate them with our thoughts.

But by what means do our actions evolve to greater perfection? To use an invariably controversial expression—how do we achieve greater perfection in our actions? We achieve this by developing in ourselves the force which can only be designated by the words: *devotion to the outer world.*—The more our devotion to the outer world grows and intensifies, the more does this outer world stir us to action. But it is just through unfolding devotion to the outer world that we succeed in permeating our actions with thoughts. What, in reality, *is* devotion to the outer world? Devotion to the outer world, which pervades our actions with thoughts, is nothing else than *love*.

Just as we attain freedom by irradiating the life of thought with will, so do we attain love by permeating the life of will with thoughts. We unfold love in our actions by letting thoughts radiate into the realm of the will; we develop freedom in our thinking by letting what is of the nature of will radiate into our thoughts. And because, as man, we are a unified whole, when we reach the point where we find freedom in the life of thought and love in the life of will, there will be freedom in our actions and love in our thinking. Each irradiates the other: action filled with thought is wrought in love; thinking that is permeated with will gives rise to actions and deeds that are truly free.

Thus you see how in man the two great ideals, Freedom and Love, grow together. Freedom and Love are also that which man, standing in the world, can bring to realization in himself in such a way that, through him, the one unites with the other for the good of the world.

We must now ask: How is the ideal, the highest ideal, to be attained in the will-permeated life of thought?—Now if the life of thought were something that represented material processes, the will could never penetrate fully into the realm of the thoughts and increasingly take root there. The will would at most be able to ray into these material processes as an organizing force. Will can take real effect only if the life of thought is something that has no outer, physical reality, if it is something that is devoid of outer, physical reality. What, then, must it be?

You will be able to envisage what it must be if you take a picture as a starting-point. If you have here a mirror and here an object, the object is reflected in the mirror; if you then go behind the mirror, you find nothing. In other words, you have a picture— nothing more. Our thoughts are pictures in this same sense. How is this to be explained?—In a previous

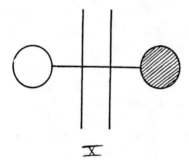

lecture I said that the life of thought *as such* is in truth not a reality of the immediate moment. The life of thought rays in from our existence before birth, or rather, before conception. The life of thought has its reality between death and a new birth. And just as here the object stands before the mirror and what it presents is a picture—only that and nothing more —so what we unfold as the life of thought is lived through in the real sense between death and a new birth, and merely rays into our life since birth. As thinking beings, we have within us a mirror-reality only. Because this is so, the other reality which, as you know, rays up from the metabolic process, can permeate the mirror-pictures of the life of thought. If, as is very rarely the case today, we make sincere endeavors to develop unbiassed thinking, it will be clear to us that the life of thought consists of mirror-pictures if we turn to thinking in its purest form—in *mathematics*. Mathematical thinking streams up entirely from our inner being, but it has a mirror-existence only. Through mathematics the make-up of external objects can, it is true, be analyzed and determined; but the mathematical thoughts in themselves are only thoughts, they exist merely as pictures. They have not been acquired from any outer reality.

Abstract thinkers such as Kant also employ an abstract expression. They say: mathematical concepts are *a priori.—A priori, apriority,* means "from what is before." * But why are mathematical concepts *a priori?* Because they stream in from the existence preceding birth, or rather, preceding conception. It is this that constitutes their 'apriority.' And the reason why they appear real to our consciousness is because they are irradiated by the will. This is what makes them real. Just think how abstract modern thinking has become when it uses abstract words for something which, in its reality, is not understood! Men such as Kant had a dim inkling that we bring mathematics with us from our existence before birth, and therefore they called the findings of mathematics 'a priori.' But the term 'a priori' really tells us nothing, for it points to no reality, it points to something merely formal.

In regard to the life of thought, which with its mirror-existence must be irradiated by the will in order to become reality, ancient traditions speak of *Semblance.* (Diagram XI, *Schein.*)

* See the *Oxford Dictionary.*

Let us now consider the other pole of man's nature, where the thoughts stream down towards the sphere of will, where deeds are performed in *love*. Here, our consciousness is so to speak held at bay, it rebounds from reality. We cannot look into that realm of darkness—a realm of darkness for our consciousness—where the will unfolds whenever we raise an arm or turn the head, unless we take supersensible conceptions to our aid. We move an arm; but the complicated process in operation there remains just as hidden from ordinary consciousness as what takes place in deep sleep, in dreamless sleep. We perceive our arm; we perceive how our hand grasps some object. This is because we permeate the action with thoughts. But the thoughts themselves that are in our consciousness are still only semblance. We live in what is real, but it does not ray into our ordinary consciousness. Ancient traditions spoke here of *Power* (*Gewalt*), because the reality in which we are living is indeed permeated by thought, but thought has nevertheless rebounded from it in a certain sense, during the life between birth and death. (Diagram XI.)

Between these two poles lies the balancing factor that unites the two—unites the will that rays towards the head with the thoughts which, as they flow into deeds wrought with love, are, so to say, felt with the heart. This means of union is the life of feeling, which is able to direct itself towards the will as well as towards the thoughts. In our ordinary consciousness we live in an element by means of which we grasp, on the one side, what comes to expression in our will-permeated thought with its predisposition to freedom, while on the other side, we try to ensure that what passes over into our deeds is filled more and more with thoughts. And what forms the bridge connecting both together has since ancient times been called: *Wisdom*. (Diagram XI.)

In his fairy-tale, *The Green Snake and the Beautiful Lily*, Goethe has given indications of these ancient traditions in the figures of the Golden King, the Silver King, and the Brazen King. We have already shown from other points of view how these three elements must come to life again, but in an entirely different form—these three elements to which ancient instinctive knowledge pointed and which can come to life again only if man acquires the knowledge yielded by Imagination, Inspiration, Intuition.

But what is it that is actually taking place as man unfolds his life of thought?—*Reality* is becoming *semblance!* It is very important to be clear about this. We carry about with us our head, which with its hard skull and tendency to ossification, presents, even outwardly, a picture of what is dead, in contrast to the rest of the living organism. Between birth and death we bear in our head that which, from an earlier time when it was reality, comes into us as semblance, and from the rest of our organism we pervade this semblance with the element issuing from our metabolic processes, we permeate it with the *real* element of the will. There we have within us a seed, a germinating entity which, first and foremost, is part of our manhood, but also means something in the cosmos. Think of it—a man is born in a particular year; before then he was in the spiritual world. When he passes out of the spiritual world, thought which there is reality, becomes semblance, and he leads over into this semblance the forces of his will which come

58

from an entirely different direction, rising up from parts of his organism other than the head. That is how the past, dying away into semblance, is kindled again to become reality of the future.

Let us understand this rightly. What happens when man rises to pure thinking, to thinking that is irradiated by will?—On the foundation of the past that has dissolved into semblance, through fructification by the will which rises up from his egohood, there unfolds within him a new reality, leading into the future. He is the bearer of the seed into the future. The thoughts of the past, as realities, are as it were the mother-soil; into this mother-soil is laid that which comes from the individual egohood, and the seed is sent on into the future for future life.

On the other side, man evolves by permeating his deeds and actions, his will-nature, with thoughts; deeds are performed in love. Such deeds detach themselves from him. Our deeds do not remain confined to ourselves. They become world-happenings; and if they are permeated by love, then love goes with them. As far as the cosmos is concerned, an egotistical action is different from an action permeated by love. When, out of semblance, through fructification by the will, we unfold that which proceeds from our inmost being, then what streams forth into the world from our head encounters our thought-permeated deeds. Just as when a plant unfolds it contains in its blossom the seed to which the light of the sun, the air outside, and so on, must come, to which something must be brought from the cosmos in order that it may grow, so what is unfolded through freedom must find an element in which to grow, through the love that lives in our deeds.

Thus does man stand within the great process of world-evolution, and what takes place inside the boundary of his skin and flows out beyond his skin in the form of deeds, has significance not only for him but for the world, the universe. He has his place in the arena of cosmic happenings, world-happenings. In that what was reality in earlier times becomes

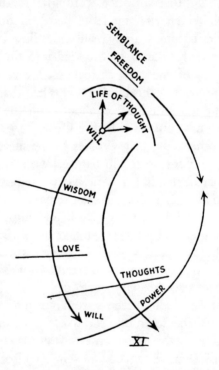

semblance in man, reality is ever and again dissolved, and in that his semblance is quickened again by the will, new reality arises. Here we have—as if spiritually we could put our very finger upon it—what has also been spoken of from other points of view.— There is no eternal conservation of matter! Matter is transformed into semblance and semblance is raised to reality by the will. The law of the conservation of matter and energy affirmed by physics is a delusion, because account is taken of the natural world only. The truth is that matter is continually passing away in that it is transformed into semblance; and a new creation takes place in that through Man, who stands before us as the supreme achievement of the cosmos, semblance is again transformed into *Being*. (*Sein*.)

We can also see this if we look at the other pole— only there it is not so easy to perceive. The processes which finally lead to freedom can certainly be grasped by unbiassed thinking. But to see rightly in the case of this other pole needs a certain degree of spiritual-scientific development. For here, to begin with, ordinary consciousness rebounds when confronted by what ancient traditions called *Power*. What is living itself out as Power, as Force, is indeed permeated by thoughts; but the ordinary consciousness does not perceive that just as more and more will, a greater and greater faculty of judgment, comes into the world of thought, so, when we bring thoughts into the will-nature, when we overcome the element of Power more and more completely, we also pervade what is merely Power with the *light* of thought. At the one pole of man's being we see the overcoming of matter; at the other pole, the new birth of matter.

As I have indicated briefly in my book, *Riddles of the Soul*, man is a threefold being: as nerves-and-senses man he is the bearer of the life of thought, of perception; as rhythmic man (breathing, circulating blood), he is the bearer of the life of feeling; as metabolic man he is the bearer of the life of will. But how, then, does the metabolic process operate in

61

man when will is ever more and more unfolded in love? It operates in that, as man performs such deeds, matter is continually overcome.—And what is it that unfolds in man when, as a free being, he finds his way into pure thinking, which is, however, really of the nature of will?—Matter is born.—We behold the coming-into-being of matter! We bear in ourselves that which brings matter to birth: our head; and we bear in ourselves that which destroys matter, where we can see how matter is destroyed: our limb-and-metabolic organism.

This is the way in which to study the *whole* man. We see how what consciousness conceives of in abstractions is an actual factor in the process of World-Becoming; and we see how that which is contained in this process of World-Becoming and to which the ordinary consciousness clings so firmly that it can do no other than conceive it to be reality—we see how this is dissolved away to nullity. It is reality for the ordinary consciousness, and when it obviously does not tally with outer realities, then recourse has to be taken to the atoms, which are considered to be firmly fixed realities. And because man cannot free himself in his thoughts from these firmly fixed realities, he lets them mingle with each other, now in this way, now in that. At one time they mingle to form hydrogen, at another, oxygen; they are merely differently grouped. This is simply because people are incapable of any other belief than that what has once been firmly fixed in thought must also be as firmly fixed in reality.

It is nothing else than feebleness of thought into which man lapses when he accepts the existence of fixed, ever-enduring atoms. What reveals itself to us through thinking that is in accordance with reality is that matter is continually dissolved away to nullity and continually rebuilt out of nullity. It is only because whenever matter dies away, new matter comes into being, that people speak of the conservation of matter. They fall into the same error into which they would fall, let us say, if a number of documents were carried into a house, copied there, but the originals burned and the copies brought out again, and then they were to believe that what was carried in has been carried out—that it is the same thing. The reality is that the old documents have been burned and new ones written. It is the same with what comes into being in the world, and it is important for our knowledge to advance to this point. For in that realm of man's being where matter dies away into semblance and new matter arises, *there* lies the possibility of freedom, and *there* lies the possibility of love. And freedom and love belong together, as I have already indicated in my *Philosophy of Spiritual Activity*.

Those who on the basis of some particular conception of the world speak of the imperishability of matter, annul freedom on the one side and the full development of love on the other. For only through the fact that in man the past dies away, becomes semblance, and the future is a new creation in the condition of a seed, does there arise in him the feeling of love—devotion to something to which he is not coerced by the past—and freedom—action that is not predetermined. Freedom and love are, in reality, comprehensible only to a spiritual-scientific conception of the world, not to any other. Those who are conversant with the picture of the world that has appeared in the course of the last few centuries will be able to assess the difficulties that will have to be overcome before the habits of thought prevailing in modern humanity can be induced to give way to this unbiassed, spiritual-scientific thinking. For in the picture of the world existing in natural science there are really no points from which we can go forward to a true understanding of freedom and love.

How the natural-scientific picture of the world on the one side, and on the other, the ancient, traditional picture of the world, are related to a truly progressive, spiritual-scientific development of humanity—of this we will speak on some other occasion.

LaVergne, TN USA
08 April 2010
178568LV00001B/4/A